SOUTHERN STEAM LOCOMOTIVE SURVEY

in the Southern Steam series

SOUTHERN STEAM LOCOMOTIVE SURVEY

BULLEID
'MERCHANT NAVY'
PACIFICS

edited by Tony Fairclough & Alan Wills

D. BRADFORD BARTON LTD

Ian Allan Ltd.

introduction

'Do you want to come into the shed to see the new engine?' —the sort of offer that no railway-minded thirteen-year-old could possibly refuse, and so it came about that the boy found himself conducted up the steps and into the Running Shed at Salisbury on a fine Sunday evening in June 1941. In his imagination he had already conjured up a vision of the locomotive he expected to see, mainly in the form of an elongated 'Lord Nelson'. His open-mouthed amazement when he clapped eyes on No.21C1 must be left to the imagination, for here was a locomotive the like of which had never before been seen on British metals. Nothing was familiar about it at all. There was the all-enveloping casing, the funny wheels, the queer number, and the cab and tender sides were *curved*! But after the first shock came the realisation of what this engine could mean. First and foremost was its immense size which dwarfed the 'King Arthurs' which stood around it. And it did have a certain beauty in its bright green livery, while its nameplate was magnificent—but, *Channel Packet*, what did it mean? Surely here was an engine which would wipe the smiles off the

faces of the Great Western supporters who had been bragging about their 'Kings' and 'Castles' for years. For the next few months, *Channel Packet* was seen venturing out on the road, but always on freight trains and unbelievable rumours were circulating that there was trouble with the new machine. On Boxing Day No.21C2 was seen thundering westwards with the morning express to Exeter but was ignominiously towed home later in the day having come off the train at Axminster with the valve gear in a mess. Little was seen of the Pacifics until March when the local lads heard that the 'cure' had been found and that No.21C3 would be working a 17-coach special from Waterloo to Exeter each day for a fortnight to give her a thorough testing. Soon after 2.00 p.m. the 'lads' gathered to see the test train climb the bank out of the city and on time and seemingly without effort, *Royal Mail* swept up the incline and away out of sight. The trials were a success, the modification having been the addition of a balancing pipe between the ends of the steam chests and in April 1942 No.21C3 went to Exmouth Junction shed, where she began working revenue earning traffic. She was soon joined by No. 21C5, painted in sombre black livery and the pair soon made their mark. Our boy's first ride behind a Bulleid is vividly recalled, not only for the ease in which a sixteen-coach train was hammered up Honiton Bank, but also for the interest shown in the locomotive by the workers in the fields alongside the line who paused in their labours to stare after the strange machine. By the end of 1942, Nos. 21C1-5 were working from Exmouth Junction and Nos. 21C6-10 from Salisbury sheds and although not yet too reliable, they proved their worth to the War Effort by their haulage of trains far in excess of anything previously attempted on the Southern. Painted in a species of refined black tar euphemistically called paint, the Pacifics could be seen tackling the banks down to Exeter or risking the death and destruction which was war-time London as they pulled away into the night bound for Waterloo. Many of the older men at Salisbury and Exeter found them difficult to handle after their straightforward 'Arthurs', but the next generation of top link drivers took to them as to the manner born and became proud of the 'Packets'. (Those who couldn't cope with them called them 'Flannel Jackets' and 'Spam Cans'!) Drivers' main complaints centred around the poor visibility which was slightly improved by the use of smoke deflectors, while the firemen had plenty to say, after they had regained enough breath, about the coal consumption of the large engines. Ten more 'Merchant Navies' appeared in 1944/5 and went to the London depot of Nine Elms; with their coming the heaviest trains on the Southern became Pacific-hauled.

The peace-time story of the famous class is unfolded in this volume. The most significant landmark came in 1956 when No. 35018 emerged from Eastleigh Works in a considerably modified form and subsequently the entire class was rebuilt in like manner. It is true to say no modern British express designs have aroused such controversy as the 'Merchant Navy' and 'West Country' classes. Praise has been showered and condemnation heaped upon these Bulleid Pacifics and neither railwaymen nor enthusiasts seem capable of considering them dispassionately and it is certain that this present work follows in that tradition. For whatever the statisticians and accountants may have to say about their maintenance costs, lbs. of coal per d.b./h.p., cost per ton/mile and other such jargon, one thing is certain —once they got going they could pull heavy express trains like the wind. During the rebuilding they lost much of the mystery and glamour which surrounded them but they continued to work with the *flaire* and *panache* which had made them engines apart. So for the writer, living with his memories, there is a debt of gratitude owing to Oliver Vaughan Snell Bulleid for having the courage to produce such a locomotive and in the mind's eye there remain vivid pictures of these great machines at work—and what happier memory of boyhood and early manhood can one have than the image of a 'Merchant Navy' storming out of Salisbury—with Father sitting in the driver's seat, hand on the regulator, watching the road ahead?

The first Bulleid Pacific, No.21C1 *Channel Packet* stands outside Eastleigh Works early in 1941 after a visit for modification. The front number plate has been lowered from the sloping section where it was originally fitted but the 'inverted horseshoe' on the smokebox remains in place. The slot above the smokebox door was designed to provide an upward draught to throw the exhaust clear of the locomotive. [H. C. Casserley collection]

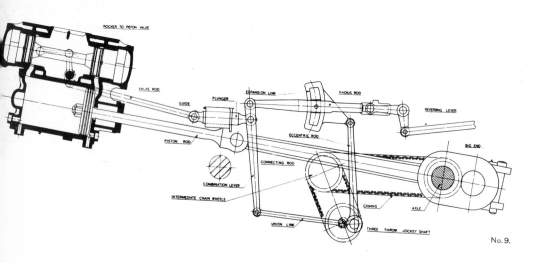

No. 9.

The 'Merchant Navy' valve gear was of Walschaerts type. In order to cut down the unsprung weight and avoid undue bulk inside the oil bath, Bulleid discarded the use of eccentrics on the crankshaft in favour of a three-throw shaft, driven from the axle by two chains, the longer of which, consisting of 118 links, each 2in in width, was over 11ft in length.

A second batch of 'Merchant Navy' 4-6-2s appeared painted in wartime austerity black livery late in 1944. Detailed variations included the smaller and flatter smoke deflectors, modified cab side sheets and the tender with an inset coal box. No. 21C14 has its nameplate *Nederland Line* fitted, but covered, ready for the naming ceremony which was eventually performed on 27 November 1945. The Pacific is hauling a heavy load of Maunsell stock through Surbiton. [L. T. George collection]

A wartime scene at Waterloo in 1945, with unnamed No. 21C19, later to be *French Line C.G.T.*, at the head of a Bournemouth line express. Nos. 21C11-20 went new to Nine Elms shed where they worked to Bournemouth and Salisbury. Until 1950 these engines were double-manned by regular crews and their footplates were scoured by the firemen, but the exterior paintwork often went uncleaned. [H. C. Casserley]

No.21C1 *Channel Packet* accelerates its fourteen-coach Sunday express up the 1 in 100 out of Templecombe on 11 May 1947. The smoke deflectors and cowl were fitted in 1943 following constant complaints from the enginemen that the exhaust obscured their vision. The horseshoe emblem was replaced by the full circle, which included the building date, after it was suggested that the horseshoe brought bad luck!

[L. T. George collection]

he gradual return to peace-time conditions in 1946 saw the repainting of the Southern's express engines in the bright alachite green livery introduced by Bulleid in the late 1930's. No.21C4 *Cunard White Star* races through Woking with down Bournemouth express on 16 September 1946, a rather unusual event, as at the time the engine belonged to xmouth Junction, whose engines then rarely penetrated to London, much less Bournemouth. However, at the time lo.21C4 was on loan to Nine Elms in exchange for No.21C14 which was undergoing coal consumption trials between xeter and Salisbury.

[Brian A. Butt]

The Southern Railway introduced glamour to its West of England lines in June 1947 when the 'Devon Belle' commenced running to Ilfracombe and Plymouth. Although booked non-stop between Waterloo and Sidmouth Junction (159 miles), the SR resorted to the subterfuge of halting the down all-Pullman express at Wilton, three miles west of Salisbury, where a Pacific from the latter shed replaced the Nine Elms engine which turned at Salisbury before returning home with the up 'Belle' from Wilton. No.21C10 *Blue Star* forges westwards near Templecombe on 19 July 1947.   [L. T. George collection]

The up train was 'Merchant Navy'-hauled between Exeter and Waterloo, with an Exmouth Junction Pacific working to Wilton where the Nine Elms engine which had come down with the 'Belle' took over for the 86 mile run to Waterloo. At that time consideration was being given to the construction of 8,000 gallon tenders so that the run would be genuinely non-stop, but the idea was not pursued and the strange spectacle continued of the vast express halted at Wilton and creeping through Salisbury at a steady 15mph! No.21C4 *Cunard White Star* hurries through Templecombe in 1947. [L. T. George collection]

In its early years, the 'Belle' was often loaded to fourteen cars, totalling some 550 tons behind the tender, and although the train was easily timed, the locomotive work had to be of a high standard in order to maintain the service. Salisbury shed was still short of cleaners in 1947, but No.21C6 *Peninsular and Oriental S.N. Co.* was well-turned out when seen near Milborne Port. The nameboard and wings added to the train's grandeur.   [L.T. George collection]

The *doyen* of the class,
No.21C1 *Channel
Packet* makes a
dramatic exit from
Exeter Central with
an express for
London. Until
February 1950 these
trains changed engines
at Salisbury;
Exmouth Junction
engines rarely
penetrated to London
in Southern Railway
days.　　[Brian A. Butt]

The locomotive exchanges of 1948 aroused intense interest throughout the country. Southern crews took 'Merchant Navy' 4-6-2s on to the Western, London Midland and Eastern Regions where they performed with distinction—if not with fuel economy. But Drivers James and Swain, of Nine Elms, ran with the *panache* associated with Southern men and were especially lively on the hilly routes, such as in South Devon and over Shap. No. 35019 *French Line C.G.T.*, complete with Stanier LMS tender (for picking up water), works the 7.50 a.m. Leeds to Kings Cross through Potters Bar on 17 May 1948.

[D. T. Cobbe]

In order to improve the forward visibility from the cab, No. 21C8 *Orient Line* was fitted with a wedge-shaped cab-front in 1947. Painted in malachite green, the engine looked particularly fine in this condition, as the cab had two full-sized side windows instead of the smaller ones which were later standardised. The first ten engines did not have the rearward facing windows at the back of the cab as did the later examples of the class, but their tenders were more shapely without the inset coal space. The Salisbury Pacific is seen at Sidmouth Junction on 15 May 1948.   [L. T. George collection]

The 'Merchant Navies' were painted Caledonian blue during the early years of British Railways. No. 35009 *Shaw Savill* approaches Buckhorn Weston Tunnel, near Gillingham with a down express on 7 April 1950. This engine went to Salisbury shed in 1942 and remained there until the mid-1950's. [L. T. George collection]

Nos. 35028-30 worked on the Eastern section boat trains during the early 1950's—the very trains for which they were first conceived. No. 35029 hurries past the chalk cliff at the Warren with the 6.10 p.m. Dover Marine to Victoria on 10 June 1950. The nameplates, *Ellerman Lines* are covered pending the naming ceremony which was held on 1 March 1951.

[D. T. Cobbe]

The curved first series tender of No. 35009 *Shaw Savill* shows up to advantage in this view, taken at Waterloo on the misty morning of 4 March 1956 as the Pacific pulls out with the 'Atlantic Coast Express'. Nos 21C3-10 were built with asbestos-fibre side sheeting in order to save weight and had the horizontal rib (for strengthening) running fore-and-aft along the boiler.   Below, immaculate second series 'Merchant Navy' No. 35017 *Belgian Marine* leads the down 'Bournemouth Belle' through the complex layout at Clapham Junction on 30 June 1956.   [A. R. Butcher]

The third series of 'Merchant Navies' was built after Nationalisation and never carried Southern Railway numbers, being Nos. 35021-30. They were very similar to the second series but had the wedge-shaped cabs and T.I.A. equipment for water treatment when built at Eastleigh between September 1948 and April 1949. No. 35022 *Holland America Line* was allocated to Exmouth Junction and is seen on shed in June 1949, painted in unlettered S R Bulleid livery.   [L. T. George collection]

The big Bulleids were invariably rostered to the heaviest duties in the 1950's. The 'Bournemouth Belle', often totalling 500 tons behind the tender, was an exacting task for Nine Elms No.1 link men. No.35011 *General Steam Navigation* swings away towards the South Coast as it heads the down 'Belle' past the Battledown Flyover at Worting Junction, Basingstoke, in July 1952.　　　　　　　　　　　　　　　　[D. T. Cobbe]

22

Exmouth Junction
Pacifics were rostered
to the up 'Atlantic Coast
Express' and from
1950 onwards worked
right through to
Waterloo. This
difficult turn was
manned by Exmouth
Junction men as far
as Salisbury, this
crew having No. 35025
Brocklebank Line for
the job on 14 August
1952. The engine had
recently received a
coat of Caledonian
blue, a livery which
suited the class quite
well when it was in
good condition.
[D. T. Cobbe]

Rarely have so many unusual features been introduced in a large production series of locomotives as were included in the Bulleid Pacific classes. Beneath the air-smoothed exterior of No.35003 *Royal Mail*, seen with the up 'A.C.E.' between Gillingham and Semley on 21 August 1958, there lay hidden the 280lbs per sq.in boiler and steel firebox which had been electrically welded, Nicholson thermic syphons and the unique chain-driven valve gear in its oil-bath actuating the outside-admission piston valves. The trailing truck with its three-point suspension gave the crew a superb ride, while the fireman's work was eased by the treadle-operated steam-powered firebox doors. Then there was the electric lighting, B.F.B. wheels and the T.I.A. water treatment. The Bulleids in their original form were beyond doubt the most technically advanced class of engines to be used extensively in Britain, and it was a great pity that they had to operate at a time when conditions of maintenance were generally against them.

[D. H. Ballantyne]

No. 35028 *Clan Line*, has
suitable decoration for
working the prestige
'Golden Arrow' at the
Warren in August 1953.
[D. T. Cobbe]

o.35027 *Port Line* works one of the boat trains for which these Pacifics were originally designed—the 20 p.m. Folkestone Harbour to Victoria, in 1954. At this date the engine, seen at Cheriton Junction, was located to Stewarts Lane shed for these heavy duties. [D. T. Cobbe]

The 12.45 p.m. Folkestone Harbour to Victoria takes the curve through Sandling behind No. 35014 *Nederland Line* on 12 July 1955. The tender has been modified, the sides having been cut down, leaving the coal bunker exposed to view. [D. T. Cobbe]

No.35021 *New Zealand Line* works its Bournemouth-bound express through Clapham Junction on 12 April 1953.

[Brian Morrison]

No.35005 *Canadian Pacific* was fitted with a Berkley mechanical stoker in March 1948 and worked in this condition until April 1950. The equipment proved successful and a higher firing rate was possible than with traditional British hand-firing but there was no saving in fuel and the experiment was not pursued. The engine is seen (at a later date, 21 May 1956) racing through Surbiton with the down 'A.C.E.'

[A. R. Butcher]

The Southern paid high regard to its milk traffic to and from the West Country and top class motive power was usually rostered to these heavy turns. The fireman of No.35005 *Canadian Pacific* looks back along the lengthy load of milk empties as his engine pulls under the distinctive gantry-mounted signal box at Clapham Junction, 25 June 1951. The headcode indicates that the train will proceed westwards via the East Putney line to Wimbledon, a route often used by the milk trains.   [Brian Morrison]

Canadian Pacific again, this time pulling out of Salisbury for Waterloo on 26 September 1958. This st
was one of the most difficult on the Western Section of the Southern, as up trains had to negotiate a t
chain curve on the rising gradient of 1 in 305 immediately on leaving the platform end. The steam san
on No.35005 is operating (on the middle pair of driving wheels) in order to gain adhesion but often
Bulleids would 'start to dance' and the most delicate handling of the stiff pull-out regulator was necess
in order to get the great engine on the move.

[P. Q. Trelo

Exmouth Junction's cleaners have worked hard on No.35003 *Royal Mail* which sparkles in the spring sun-
shine as she heads a thirteen-coach load from Exeter out of Basingstoke on 17 April 1957.   [A. R. Butcher]

A final look at *Channel Packet* in its largely original condition. The valance between the cylinders and buffer beam has been cut away to allow for easier access to the steam chests, and of course the smoke deflectors and wedge-shaped cab which had become standard are evident, but otherwise the machine is still an authentic 'Bulleid'. The shutters on the tender are visible in this view (taken at Eastleigh, 18 April 1956), these having been fitted for blackout purposes during the War. The high platform under the smokebox door made the task of cleaning out the box rather unpleasant, as the fireman was working up amongst the fumes which were emitted from the boiler tubes. The mechanical lubricators were fitted beneath this platform, a position which allowed ash to penetrate to those vital components.   [A. R. Butcher]

A 'Merchant Navy' defrocked. No. 35013 *Blue Funnel* followed sisters Nos. 35018/20 into Eastleigh works in the early months of 1956 to undergo the extensive modifications which completely altered the appearance of the engines as well as changing many of their distinctive mechanical features. Some final adjustment are being made to the Pacific on 25 July 1956.

[Brian Morrison

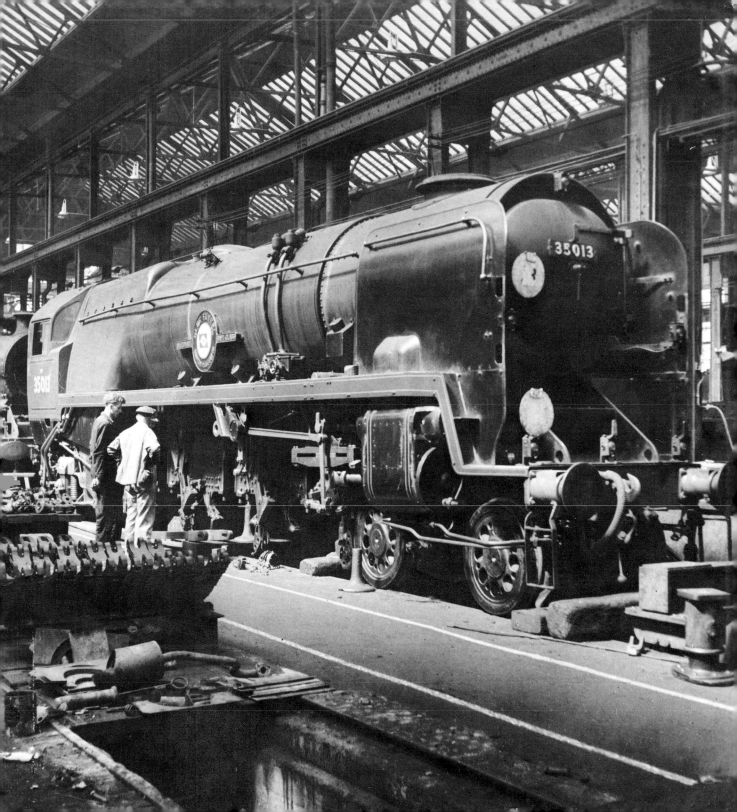

In order to improve the fuel consumption and general reliability of the 'Merchant Navies', the Southern Region's Chief Technical Assistant (Locomotives), R. G. Jarvis, initiated the modifications, the detailed design of which was performed at the Brighton drawing offices. The Pacific now had a conventional appearance and was considered quite handsome by many students of locomotives' looks. The first engine to be modified, No. 35018 *British India Line* is seen outside its home shed, Nine Elms, on 6 October 1957.

[A. E. Bennett]

No. 35013 *Blue Funnel* eases down towards the Nine Elms turntable on 6 October 1957. Below, another rebuilt 'Merchant Navy' was on view at Nine Elms that day. The substitution of three sets of Walschaerts valve gear for the controversial Bulleid gear in its oil bath solved certain problems, but it reintroduced a great deal more oiling for the drivers, and No. 35022 *Holland America Line* is receiving the traditional attention with the oil can before making a run home to Bournemouth.

[A. E. Bennett]

The rebuilds were soon put to work on the principal express turns, where their performance was closely watched by railwaymen and enthusiasts alike. They proved to be extremely capable express motive power and settled into the work to the West Country without fuss or failures. No.35020 *Bibby Line* hurtles out of Buckhorn Weston Tunnel towards Templecombe with a west-bound express on 10 September 1960.

[G. A. Richardson]

No. 35003 *Royal Mail* storms up the bank towards Semley with an east-bound holiday relief on 20 August 1960. Gone are the days when the drivers had to peer through clouds of exhaust with the 'originals' as the smoke deflectors of the 'rebuilds' served their purpose admirably, as this view shows.

[G. A. Richardson]

The impressive front-end view of No. 35018 *British India Line* as seen from an up local on 2 October 1957. The scene is Vauxhall, the first station out of Waterloo and the Pacific is just getting into her stride after the usual slow exit away from the terminus.

[A. R. Butcher]

The last of the 'Merchant Navies', No. 35030 *Elder-Dempster Lines*, emerged from Eastleigh Works in April 1949. Exactly nine years later she appeared in modified form, and continued in service for yet another nine years, lasting to the *finale* of steam in July 1967. The Nine Elms locomotive is seen at Tisbury Gates, three stations west of Salisbury, on 21 August 1958.

[D. H. Ballantyne]

The pioneer Rebuild, No. 35018 *British India Line*, had been in service for just two months when it was photographed at Surbiton in charge of the twelve-car 'Bournemouth Belle', 21 May 1956. The superb Bulleid boiler, the best feature of the original design, was retained on the rebuild, although the pressure was lower at 250lbs per sq.in, and with this as the heart of the locomotive, the modified design was ensured success.

[A. R. Butcher]

Bournemouth's 'Merchant Navy' Pacifics did not receive the best of attention during the run-down of steam in the 1960's, but some wonderful performances were recorded on this line in the twilight years. No.35027 *Port Line* passes Wimbledon with the Pullman train on 9 March 1964.

[P. J. Lynch]

he 'Bournemouth Belle' was always one of the main show cases for 'Merchant Navy' performance. Often aded to twelve Pullmans or some 500 tons behind the tender, the schedule of 81 minutes for the 79 miles o Southampton Central allowed no time for dawdling. Bournemouth men were responsible for handling his turn in the late 1950's and 1960's. This view shows No. 35011 *General Steam Navigation* approaching asingstoke on 10 June 1965.

[P. J. Lynch]

clear road through Basingstoke for the down 'Belle' on 17 April 1957 with No.35010 *Blue Star* at the head f the immaculate rake of Pullmans.

[A. R. Butcher]

A late-afternoon express for Bournemouth starts away from Waterloo behind No.35026 *Lamport and Holt Line* on 19 October 1957. The climb out of the terminus made a difficult start for the light-footed Bulleids as the use of the steam sanders was not much encouraged because of the danger of interference with the electric track-circuiting.

[A. E. Bennett]

At Bournemouth, 108 miles down the line from Waterloo, No.35024 *East Asiatic Company*, emits a plume of steam in the autumn sky as she blows off with a shattering roar while waiting for departure time with a Weymouth to Waterl express, September 1962. Engines were usually changed at Bournemouth on the through Weymouth trains, the Ni Elms and Bournemouth crews making out-and-home trips of 216 miles, the longest regular rosters on Southern meta

[G. A. Richardso

The gun-metal nameplates were among the most handsome fitted to British locomotives. The sheet metal centrepiece sported the house flag of the shipping company concerned and each side had the flag flying in the appropriate direction.

[D. T. Cobbe]

There were many variations among the thirty tenders attached to the rebuilt 'Merchant Navies'. No. 35026 *Lamport and Holt Line* has a 6,000 gallon long-wheelbase tender with a large canopy, covering the vacuum reservoirs, prominent at the rear of the coal space, which has been stacked full as the Pacific leaves Waterloo for Bournemouth in the summer of 1957.
                                                                    [A. R. Butcher]

'Merchant Navy' 4-6-2 No. 35016 *Elders Fyffes* on view at Bournemouth (West) with smaller 'West Country' cousin No. 34105 *Swanage* drifting into the platform with the down 'Pines Express'. Although the smaller Pacifics could perform wonders when pressed, they did not have the reserves of power available to the 'Merchant Navies' and were usually rostered to the easier turns.   [G. A. Richardson]

There was a certain family resemblance between the rebuilt Bulleids and the Standard 'Britannia' Pacifics, as is evident in this scene taken at Bournemouth (Central) on 8 March 1964. The similarity was obtained by the design of such components as the running plates, cabs, reversing gear and smoke deflectors, but the mechanical concept of the two designs was very different. The Standards were essentially simple, straight-forward common-user workhorses, while the Bulleids were thoroughbreds. No. 35028 *Clan Line* is arriving with the up 'Bournemouth Belle' as No. 70020 *Mercury* waits to go on shed to turn before working an enthusiasts' special to Waterloo.   [G. A. Richardson]

'Merchant Navy' Pacifics, seen amidst the winter's snow west of Salisbury on the down 'Atlantic Coast Express' during the bitterest weather experienced for the decade. The bullocks stand unmoved as No. 35030 *Elder-Dempster Lines*, wreathed in steam, thunders past up the 1 in 144 gradient out of Wilton in February 1963. Above, No. 35015 *Rotterdam Lloyd* roars downhill past Chilmark, west of Wilton, with the down 'Atlantic Coast Express' in the same month. In very frosty weather, the exhaust tended to cling around the short chimneys of the rebuilt Bulleids, but the smoke deflectors could be relied upon to lift the steam clear of the cab windows.   [G. A. Richardson]

On to highsummer, 1963, with No. 35012 *United States Lines* forging ahead up the bank from Wilton with a down relief. Bulleid designed his Pacifics so that they could be driven from a sitting position and the driver has adopted the attitude usually maintained by 'Merchant Navy' enginemen. This view shows clearly the very narrow step and running plate alongside the smoke deflectors, an unpopular feature of the engine which made the carrying of oil bottles and sand most awkward for the preparation men.

[G. A. Richardson]

No. 35020 *Bibby Line* in full cry with a West of England express. The front-end design, with large exhaust ports, short piston-stroke (24in) and the excellent steam passage layout made these engines extremely free running. The fastest recorded speed was 104 mph, attained near Gillingham, but many other instances of 'the ton' were recorded over the years.

[G. A. Richardson]

Salisbury's No. 35006 *Peninsular and Oriental S.N. Co.*, built in January 1942, was modified in October 1959, and continued on its shed's 'Merchant Navy' roster until September 1964, when the West Country services were reorganised and the big Pacifics were replaced by Western Region 'Warship' diesels. Unfortunately No. 35006 was then sent to the scrap-heap. However, on 2 June 1962 it was working one of Salisbury's freight turns and is seen heaving its load over the summit at the mouth of Buckhorn Weston Tunnel. Although classified as mixed-traffics during the War years, they were largely used on express turns in later years. [G. A. Richardson]

No. 35006 pulls out of Sidmouth Junction on 13 July 1963, working one of its regular duties, the 8.00 a.m. Salisbury t[o] Exeter slow. Salisbury No. 1 link men worked this train to Exeter (returning with the up 'Brighton') but the engine worke[d] the 2.30 p.m. Exeter to Waterloo, with an Exmouth Junction crew to Salisbury, where another Salisbury Top Link pa[ir] of men took her up to Waterloo, returning home with the 10.15 p.m. non-stop fitted freight, an extremely arduous tur[n] which taxed the firemen to the full. [W. L. Underha[y]

54

The late 1950's were good years on the Southern. The maintenance of track and express locomotives had regained some semblance of pre-war standards and, as yet, no shadows from the forthcoming Beeching Axe dimmed the enthusiasm of serving railwaymen who believed in their work and in themselves. No. 35013 *Blue Funnel* steams proudly through Semley on 21 August 1958 with the 8·25 a.m. from Plymouth. In less than ten years, the Pacific will have disappeared along with all other BR steam locomotives, while the Southern's route to the West will be a shadow of its former self.

[D. H. Ballantyne]

57

Mighty 'Merchant Navy' Pacific No. 35014 *Nederland Line* waits quietly in the yard at Seaton Junction after its 148-mile trip from Waterloo with the 10.45 p.m. to Seaton, 14 July 1962. The through Saturdays-only express has been taken down the branch and No. 35014 is waiting for a pathway through to Exmouth Junction shed. With a succession of express trains having to clear the formidable section over Honiton bank, finding a path for a light engine was not easy and No. 35014 was still waiting as No. 35026 *Lamport and Holt Line* slightly eases its headlong flight down the bank to observe the 60 mph speed restriction through the station as it approaches with the 11.45 a.m. Bude to Waterloo.

[W. L. Underhay]

Power personified—No. 35004 *Cunard White Star* charges the bank out of Templecombe with the 1.00 p.m. from Waterloo on 4 November 1961. This Pacific went new to Exmouth Junction but moved to Salisbury about 1948, remaining there until the major reshuffle of September 1964 when it was transferred to Bournemouth. The engine is working another of Salisbury's 'Merchant Navy' turns—the 8.15 a.m. Salisbury to Waterloo, then the 1.00 p.m. Waterloo to Exeter with Salisbury No. 1 Link men down as far as their home station, relieved by Exmouth Junction men returning home. The engine regained Salisbury on the 7.45 p.m. Mail from Exeter.

[G. A. Richardson]

An easy job for No. 35010 *Blue Star* as it moves effortlessly out of Wilton (South) on the last lap of its run up from Exeter with an all-stations 'stopper' on 30 July 1961. The big Pacifics often worked such filling-in duties in the West of England between more exacting spells of duty.

[D. H. Ballantyne]

Nos. 35014 *Nederland Line* and 35017 *Belgian Marine* have worked down from Waterloo on 28 August 19
and now stand on the pits at Exmouth Junction. On the right is the large coal hopper, which many m
alleged smashed up the coal more than the Nine Elms structure. Old enginemens' tale or no, it was wide
believed by men from visiting depots.

[A. R. Butche

The 'Merchant Navies' were not allowed to proceed beyond Exeter (Central), having an axle loading of over 21 tons, so the sight of these Pacifics backing up the line towards Exmouth Junction shed was a familiar one to travellers in the city. The recently overhauled No. 35024 *East Asiatic Company* has come off the 9.00 a.m. from Waterloo and will return home to London with the 4.30 p.m. from Exeter. Train crews liked the operations at Central because they were rarely kept waiting around the station precincts after coming off the down trains, but were invariably signalled away to shed as quickly as possible.

[J. R. Besley]

The Merchant Navy theme was chosen for Bulleid's first design at a time when that gallant service was much in the war-time public eye. The actual names may not have been particularly inspiring but they commemorated famous international companies.

[Brian Morrison]

The 'Merchant Navies' worked through to Oxford with inter-Regional turns such as the 'Pines Express' which is seen pulling out of Southampton Central towards the tunnel behind No. 35027 *Port Line* in May 1966.   [T. P. Cooper]

'The shades lengthen and the evening comes, the busy world is hushed, the fever of life is over, and our work is done'—but not the work of the Nine Elms men on No. 35017 *Belgian Marine*, for while the worthy citizens of Southampton are gathering around their firesides, these footplatemen have 79 miles of hard running and two tons of coal-shovelling ahead of them before they get relief at Waterloo, some ninety minutes later. The fireman has built up a good fire and a full head of steam in preparation for the slogging climb to Litchfield Tunnel, some 22 miles away. [D. M. Cox]

A close-up of No.35023 *Holland-Afrika Line* at Templecombe, 28 March 1965. On the extreme lower right can be seen the $\frac{3}{4}$ hp turbo-generator which supplied the electricity for the head lights, cab illumination and inspection lights. The shiny box above the turbine contains the electrical fuses. Footholds were cut into the lower cab sheets so that the men could climb on to the running plates. The trailing truck was one of the successes of the original design and was adopted by BR for its Standard Pacific designs. The ashpan of the Rebuild was redesigned as a self-emptying type, with a rocker grate above it. The speedometer was fitted in the 1960's and perhaps proved too much of a temptation to the men to have a 'last fling' when conditions were right! [D. T. Cobbe]

A down Bournemouth express pauses at Brockenhurst on 13 May 1966 with No. 35026 *Lamport and Holt Line* at the head. The Pacific's boiler appears to be of parallel design, but in fact it has a taper on the underside, contrary to the usual British practice. The first ten engines had the taper on the first ring, the later series on the second. It will be noted that both injectors are on the fireman's side, a Bulleid innovation which was much appreciated. Probably no one had ever though of such a thing before!   [D. M. Cox]

No. 35014 *Nederland Line* stands at Salisbury on New Year's Day 1964 as Standard Class '5' 4-6-0 No. 73044 comes in with a freight from Western Region. The two Wakefield mechanical lubricators for the left hand cylinders can be seen to the rear of the smoke deflector. The leading sand box is adjacent. The pipe running along the boiler supplies steam to the blower which is used for drawing up the fire when the regulator is closed.

[G. A. Richardson]

An opportunity to study the front of No.35003 *Royal Mail* as she stands in Bournemouth shed on 8 November 1964, her new home after a move from Exmouth Junction in September 1964. The original Bulleid fabricated smokebox had been replaced by an orthodox cylindrical model resting on a saddle but the familiar eliptical door was retained. A flared cast iron chimney, much heavier than the original stovepipe, was placed above the retained Lemaitre blast pipe. The cleaning of the smoke-box was somewhat eased by having the front platform in a lower position (see page 32). Immediately to the rear of the right hand deflector may be seen the Silvertown mechanical lubricator for the axle-boxes with the third Wakefield for the right-hand cylinder. The code 70F replaced the more familiar 71B for Bournemouth in 1962, and AWS equipment was fitted about the same time.

[Philip D. Hawkins]

Most drivers of 'Merchant Navies' spent their working lives peering out of the side windows along the large boiler, anxious to catch their first glimpse of the vital signals as they hurtled along the main lines. There can be no doubt that the biggest improvement for the footplatemen due to the rebuilding was in the visibility from the cab, as the rebuilds did not suffer from the problems of drifting exhaust which so bedevilled the originals. The running plate of No. 35011 *General Steam Navigation*, seen at Templecombe on 1 January 1966, looks greasy and slippery and care will have to be taken when walking along the narrow plating. It is incredible to think that old-time enginemen took a pride in walking to the front when their engines were in motion in order to lubricate the works.

[N. E. Preedy]

A peep into the holy of holies, the footplate, which for most people was forbidden territory. The fireman has built up his fire on No. 35012 *United States Lines* ready for the run to Bournemouth with the 2.30 p.m. from Waterloo and the tea has been brewed and cups placed ready for action. The needle on the boiler pressure gauge, seen through the rear spectacle, shows that pressure is just under blowing off point at 250lbs per sq.in, so she is ready to roll. The 'Merchant Navy' cabs were comfortable, though dust was liable to be trapped inside, and the controls were well placed. On the driver's side were the pull-out regulator, brake handle, reverser, blower, steam chest pressure gauge, oil pressure gauges, cylinder cock levers and a water level glass. On the right were the two injectors, boiler pressure and steam heating gauges, dampers, pet-pipe (for watering the coal) and the second water level column.

[J. R. Besley]

An up Bournemouth express disdainfully passes Raynes Park in the late 1950's with recently rebuilt No. 35002 *Union Castle* showing her paces at the head of a mixed rake of stock. Long and unresolved arguments have continued among the footplatemen as to the relative merits of the two versions of the class. It was generally conceded that the rebuilds were more reliable, the visibility was certainly far superior, and certain details such as the reverser, were improved, but for the drivers there was the additional oiling of the valve gear. Many men felt that the originals were stronger, and although the Bulleid boiler remained unchanged, it was widely considered that the rebuilds took longer to steam freely, whereas the original engines steamed superbly as soon as the regulator was opened and the blast hit the fire.

[A. R. Butcher]

Another view, near Christchurch, of the down 'Bournemouth Belle', this time hauled by No.35011 *General Steam Navigation*. The number 385 on the disc is the locomotive duty number, this being one of the series allotted to Bournemouth shed, and the position of the discs indicate that the train is running on the Waterloo-Bournemouth route.

[G. A. Richardson]

Engine and Pullmans look in splendid condition as the 'Belle' pulls out of Southampton behind No. 35002 *Union Castle* on 1 September 1962. The withdrawal of the Pullman train in July 1967 deprived the Bournemouth line of its old world glamour service.

[D. T. Cobbe]

Salisbury was the station *par excellence* for studying the 'Merchant Navy' Pacifics. Before 1950, all trains changed engines here, but following the introduction of the through workings between Waterloo and Exeter, the Pacifics were remanned and serviced at the platform. Only six minutes were allowed in the working timetables for taking on 5,000 gallons of water, shovelling coal forward and relieving the crew. No. 35007 *Aberdeen Commonwealth*, of Salisbury shed, is unusually working the 9.00 a.m. from Waterloo (a Nine Elms turn) and the Nine Elms men are being relieved by the Exmouth Junction pair who came up to Salisbury with the 7.30 a.m. from Exeter earlier in the day. The 'W' is attached to a post and acted as a marker to enable the driver to stop opposite the water column.

[G. A. Richardson]

Salisbury shed often posted young firemen on the station platforms to help shovel coal forward during the time allowed for taking water on the through trains. No.35013 *Blue Funnel* stands at the head of the up 'Atlantic Coast Express' at the top end of No.2 Platform on 18 April 1964. The Salisbury No. 1 ('Main Line') Link driver is about to mount the footplate to take over from the Exmouth Junction man who has come up from Exeter. The Salisbury man will work home with the 7.00 p.m. from Waterloo while the Exeter crew will take on the 3.00 p.m. ex-Waterloo from Salisbury at 4.45 p.m. The five tons of coal carried was just sufficient for the through run of 171 miles, but the 5,100 gallons of some of the tenders was rather tight for the 83 miles to Waterloo, whereas the 6,000 gallon tenders relieved the drivers of much of their anxiety.

[D. H. Ballantyne]

Although Salisbury shed lost its allocation of 'Merchant Navies' in September 1964, the big engines were still to be seen on shed in the ensuing years. No. 35017 *Belgian Marine* looks particularly smart as she comes off the pits on 23 May 1965.

[D. T. Cobbe]

Bournemouth-based No. 35027 *Port Line* comes off the coal road at Nine Elms shed in October 1964.

[A. R. Butcher]

The 'Atlantic Coast Express' from Waterloo races down the 1 in 170 bank towards Milborne Port with No. 35026 *Lamport and Holt Line* in charge. The engine exhibits a characteristic of the maintenance of the class—that is the patch of dirt along the top of the boiler. The cleaners, standing on the running plates, could almost reach to the top of the boiler, but not quite, hence the streak of grime!

[G. A. Richardson]

The Okehampton to Surbiton car-carrier accelerates away from Exeter (Central) towards Blackboy Tunnel on 3 August 1963. Class 8 power has been rostered to the turn in the shape of No. 35016 *Elders Fyffes*, which has been given a good clean for the trip.

[W. L. Underhay]

A further view of a Salisbury Pacific on 'The One O'Clock', the 1.00 p.m. from Waterloo to the West of England, taken on 8 June 1964, shortly before the locomotive diagrams were recast. No. 35004 *Cunard White Star* tops the long rise to Semley station with visible evidence from the chimney of the fireman's hard work. The 'Merchant Navies' were pretty heavy on coal, the rebuilds being slightly more economical in this respect. [Derek Cross]

While the civil engineers had possession of the down main line during the electrification works, the unusual sight of huge Pacifics hammering up the single-line Medstead bank inspired many photographers to produce some of their best locomotive portraits. On 1 May 1966 No. 35008 *Orient Line* was caught at the head of the 10.30 a.m. Waterloo to Weymouth as she was attacking the 1 in 60 incline. [M. J. Fox]

No. 35011 *General Steam Navigation* ventured on to Somerset & Dorset metals on 1 January 1966 when it was commissioned to work an enthusiasts' tour. The 4-6-2 is seen on shed at Templecombe, where it was coaled by hand from wagons alongside.

[D. M. Cox]

The same locomotive, No. 35011, enjoying its final overhaul in Eastleigh Works on 6 March 1965. Although a 'Battle of Britain' can be seen in the background, the Bulleid is surrounded by alien types, including ex-LMS 2-8-0 No. 48671 which, strangely enough was built by the Southern Railway at its Ashford Works in 1943, some eighteen months before the Pacific was constructed. A close study of the photograph shows various interesting bits and pieces of locomotives, including boiler tubes, steam chest covers, and motion, plus a snow plough in the middle road.   [D. M. Cox]

Although the Pacifics were designed and, later, redesigned at the Brighton Drawing Offices, the 'Merchant Navies' rarely appeared in that area; No. 35007 *Aberdeen Commonwealth* makes a welcome sight in Brighton station on 18 October 1964, having worked in with a special from Littlehampton.

[A. R. Butcher]

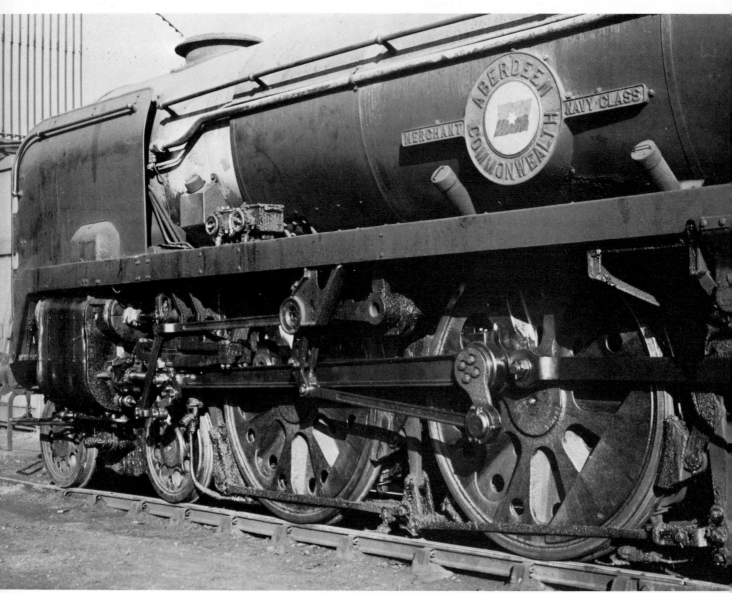

The Jarvis version of Walschaerts gear on rebuilt No. 35007 *Aberdeen Commonwealth*. The Bulleid chain-driven gear in its oil batch was the most controversial feature of the original design, and when the modification of the Pacifics was considered, that valve gear was the first thing to go. The original outside cylinders were re-used while a new inside cylinder and steam chest were provided. The fluted coupling rods have been replaced by plain rectangular components, while balance weights have appeared on the driving wheels. The filler pipes for the three left-hand sand boxes stand out above the running plate. The 'Merchant Navies' were fitted with clasp brakes, the shoes acting on either side of each driving wheel, whose 6ft 2in diameter proved no handicap to the speed potential of these flyers.   [N. E. Preedy]

No. 35026 *Lamport and Holt Line* arouses great interest as she stands, far from home, in Newcastle Central on 22 October 1966. North Eastern men crewed her on a special from York to Newcastle, and on the return journey worked their strange mount up to 90 mph on this level route.

[John Chalcraft]

An express coming
up to Town from
Bournemouth at full
speed on the up local
near Milepost 31,
two miles east of
Farnborough, June
1965, with No. 35027
Port Line as motive
power. The fireman is
having a breather, and
can now let his fire
die down, for the train
faces a steady downhill
run to the terminus.
Well might he take it
easy, for that first
31 miles out of
Waterloo on the way
home will tax his
strength to the full,
and all express crews
were glad to be over
that summit on the
downward run,
especially with an
engine which had
come 'cold' off Nine
Elms shed.
        [A. R. Butcher]

With less than a week of steam working to go, No. 35007, without its *Aberdeen Commonwealth* nameplate, still looks neat and tidy as she stands in steam inside Nine Elms shed on 4 July 1967. This great depot, with its long tradition of hard running, closed down at the end of steam working, but it maintained Bulleid Pacifics to the end.   [D. M. Cox]

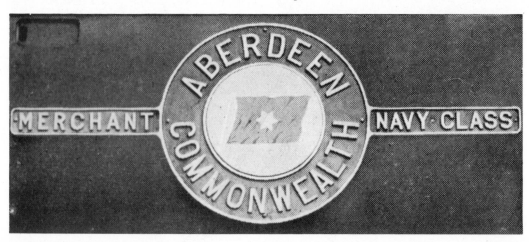

The
missing nameplate

For long a stronghold of Great Western classes, Weymouth shed—once the home of 'Saints', 'Stars' and 'Halls'—found itself with several mighty 'Merchant Navies' and 'West Countries' on its books after September 1964. These engines were used on the through turns to London, which had all been routed to Waterloo instead of sharing the traffic with Paddington. The Pacifics were not very well maintained during those final years of steam, yet they still performed magnificently. No. 35030 *Elder-Dempster Lines* stands ready for duty on 1 May 1966.   [Philip D. Hawkins]

The 'third rails' are in position alongside the continuously welded track, and steam is having its last fling. No.35028 *Clan Line* has been thoroughly cleaned for working one of the Southern's 'Last Steam Specials', the 4.30 p.m. Bournemouth (Central) to Waterloo on 2 July 1967, and is rousing the echoes as it pounds up the long pull at 1 in 251 to Litchfield Tunnel. [D. T. Cobbe]

A final look at a handsome 'Merchant Navy' nameplate. With the lettering polished and the red-painted background cleaned up, these plates were splendidly decorative. [T. P. Cooper]

Put the pipe in, turn on the water, shovel the coal forward—for the last time, for the date is 8 July 1967, the final day of steam running in the Southern Region. Apart from some specials on the following day (Sunday), the reign of the Southern steam locomotive was ending, and many enthusiasts were present for the last rites. For the footplatemen, the hard physical work also will be largely eliminated, to be replaced by the strain of high-speed electric running which can be just as taxing to the drivers. Although the 'Merchant Navies' are no longer at work, all thirty are recorded for posterity in this Survey.   [P. J. Lynch]

First the melodious 'Middle C' of the Bulleid's whistle is heard as the 'Atlantic Coast Express' rounds the curves through Wilton station, then the sparkling green-liveried 'Merchant Navy' appears in view at the foot of the bank. With the exhaust crackling, the locomotive thunders nearer, and with a courteous nod from the grizzled Exmouth Junction veteran seated in the cab, No. 35010 *Blue Star* sweeps past, motion clanking and the music from the chimney rising to a tumultuous crescendo. And in that brief moment, the observer is given a fleeting glimpse of that supreme vision of 'watching trains', the sight of the fireman as he deftly swings his coal-laden shovel into the incandescent glare of the firebox. It is upon his stamina, skill and willingness that the burden of working locomotive and train depends. Then the Pacific is under the bridge and away round the curve and as the passengers glide past in cushioned comfort, the observer hears the blast sharpen perceptibly, and he sees, in his mind's eye, the reproachful look on the begrimed face of the hard-pressed fireman as the unrelenting driver heaves the regulator handle up to the roof, gives the reverser a couple of turns and lengthens the cut-off yet again.

[G. A. Richardson]

Hundreds of men helped to build you, hundreds more maintained you and worked on your footplate ... They hated you, cursed you, loved you and will remember you with affection ... Many footplatemen from Exmouth Junction, Salisbury, Nine Elms, Bournemouth, Eastleigh, Stewarts Lane and Dover found fame at your regulator and became the heroes of the railway press. Many more made equally wonderful runs and remained unsung, but are remembered by their colleagues for their prowess fully deserving the simple epithet of being 'good enginemen'. They knew, through long experience, how to make you pick up your heels and go, when lesser mortals could not handle such mettlesome mounts as you and your twenty-nine stable companions. Once you could run at 100 mph or pull 600 tons, now you are no longer No. 35010 *Blue Star* but just so much rusting scrap metal in Woodham Brothers' Yard in alien South Wales. This is not the 'Merchant Navy' we knew and as for so many of those who worked on you, retirement has come, and for you, it could have been with more dignity.

[M. J. Jackson]

Thanks to the valiant efforts of the 'Merchant Navy' Locomotive Preservation Society, No. 35028 *Clan Line* has been beautifully restored to full working order and has made several successful forays out on the main lines. The first major outing was on an excursion from Basingstoke to Westbury and back on 27 April 1974. Gleaming in a new coat of paint, *Clan Line* makes a splendid picture as it prepares for the return run from Westbury.

[J. R. Besley]

Once more the tinny rasp of a 'Merchant Navy' exhaust is heard at Salisbury, as No. 35028 *Clan Line*, on its return journey, makes her careful exit from No. 2 Platform as in the days of yore. With the driver opening and shutting the regulator so that she will keep her feet and the fireman ready to apply the steam sander, it seems as if the years have rolled back. Although the restored Pacific's finest hour so far has undoubtedly been its appearance in the Grand Cavalcade at Shildon on 31 August 1975, yet it is appropriate that this volume, which began its survey at Salisbury, should close in the same Wiltshire city.

[J. R. Besley]